Preschool Pro

My First Songbook
Volume I
by Robert and Samantha Young

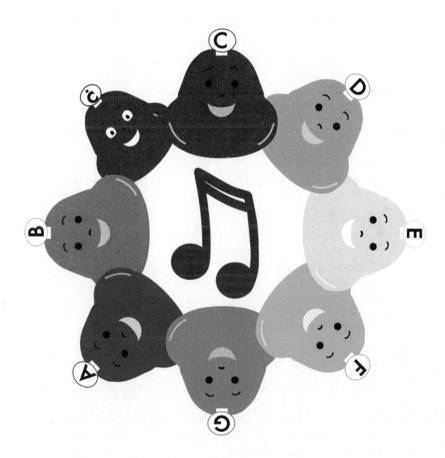

Production: Robert and Samantha Young
Cover and Illustrations: Robert Young with art licensed at FreePik.com
Printed by: Amazon CreateSpace

ISBN 978-1519520074

Table of Contents

Welcome to _____ Songbook
(first name)

In this book, you will sing and play songs with eight (8) musical notes.

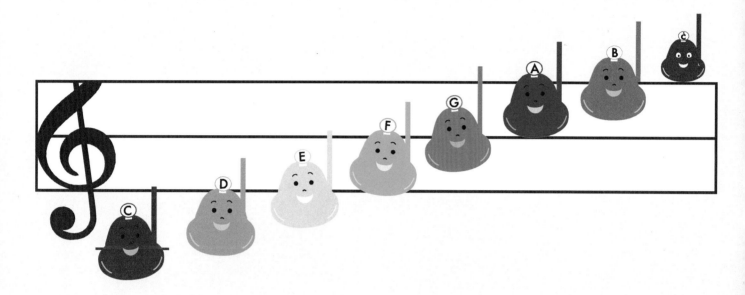

Try playing the notes above! Start on the left, just like when you read any book, and you work your way to the right.

The colorful notes help make reading the music easier and more fun!

By reading music like this, you can sing and play songs like Mary Had a Little Lamb and Twinkle Twinkle Little Star.

If you have an instrument, start by just playing the song on your instrument.

After you've played the songs on your instrument, trying singing the words to the song as you play along!

After that, you can practice with Solfege hand signs, which will help improve your singing and your sense of pitch.

You won't use all the notes in every song! To figure out what notes you need, look for a picture like this one at the beginning of a song.

Notes Used:

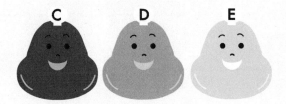

Those are the notes you'll need for that song! Try to set your bells up just like the picture.

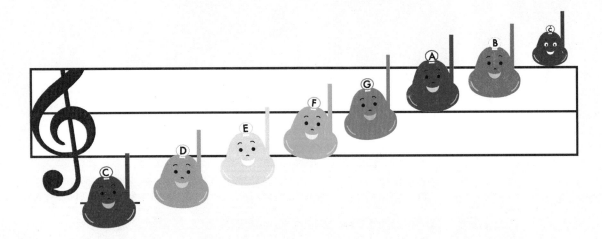

Did you notice that there are two (2) red bells named C?

We have one C at the beginning and another at the end! This is because the musical notes repeat in a pattern.

High Notes and Low Notes

Do you remember how many notes we have? Count them if you forgot!

The lowest note is the big C Bell. Do you see how it sits lower than all the other notes?

As you go from note C to note D, you are stepping up and getting higher. You can keep stepping up to higher and higher notes, until you hit the top of pattern at little belll c.

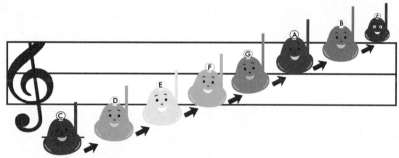

Then from the little bell c, you can step all the way back down to the low C.

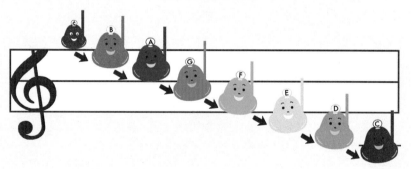

These notes live inside the treble clef and in this book, we will work with a small section of the treble clef!

How Long are the Notes?

A blank musical space is called a measure.

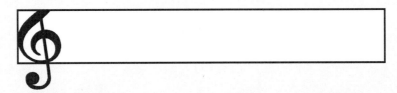

The measures in this book all have four (4) beats!

The whole note gets four (4) beats and takes up a whole measure.

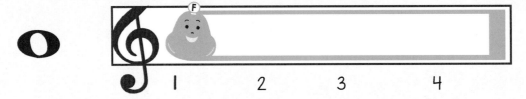

The half note gets two (2) beats and takes up half the measure.

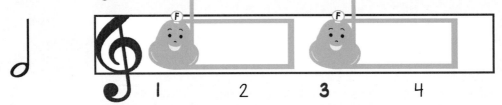

The quarter note gets one (1) beat and takes up one-quarter of the measure.

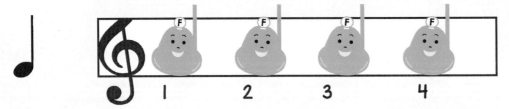

The eighth note gets one-half (1/2) of a beat and takes up one-eighth of the measure.

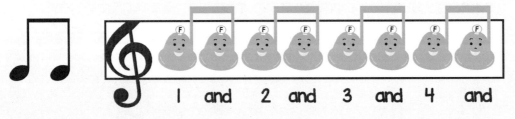

The Solfege Hand Signs

Not only can you play and sing along with the songs in this book, but you can hand-sign along with the different musical notes.

Hand-signing along is a great way to make sure you are singing the right note.

By signing along with the notes, you will begin to memorize the sounds of notes much faster.

When we hand sign, we sing with syallabels we call Solfege. The Solfege syllabels are "do re mi fa sol la ti and do."

When you sing "do," you turn your hands into fists near your waist. The symbols on the right show you the hand signs and their Solfege syllable.

Learn about the rest of the Solfege hand symbols by visiting **preschoolprodigies.com/course.**

Use the password **musictime** to jump in singing and hand-signing with Mr. Rob.

BONUS: Companion Video Course

This book comes with companion videos to help make playing the songs even easier!

Learn more about the Solfege hand signs, playing in time and where the notes live in the treble clef at

PreschoolProdigies.com/course

password:

musictime

I hope you enjoy the songbook and the companion videos!

This is the upteenth rendition of this book, and I really hope you love it as much as we do! Volume II is almost complete, so if you enjoy this book, check out Volume II!

Next time you're on Pinterest, YouTube, Facebook, etc.... look us up and say hi! We'll make you laugh, help your kids fall in love with music and definitely not blow up your feed in the process.

Until next time...

Mr. Rob

Hot Cross Buns

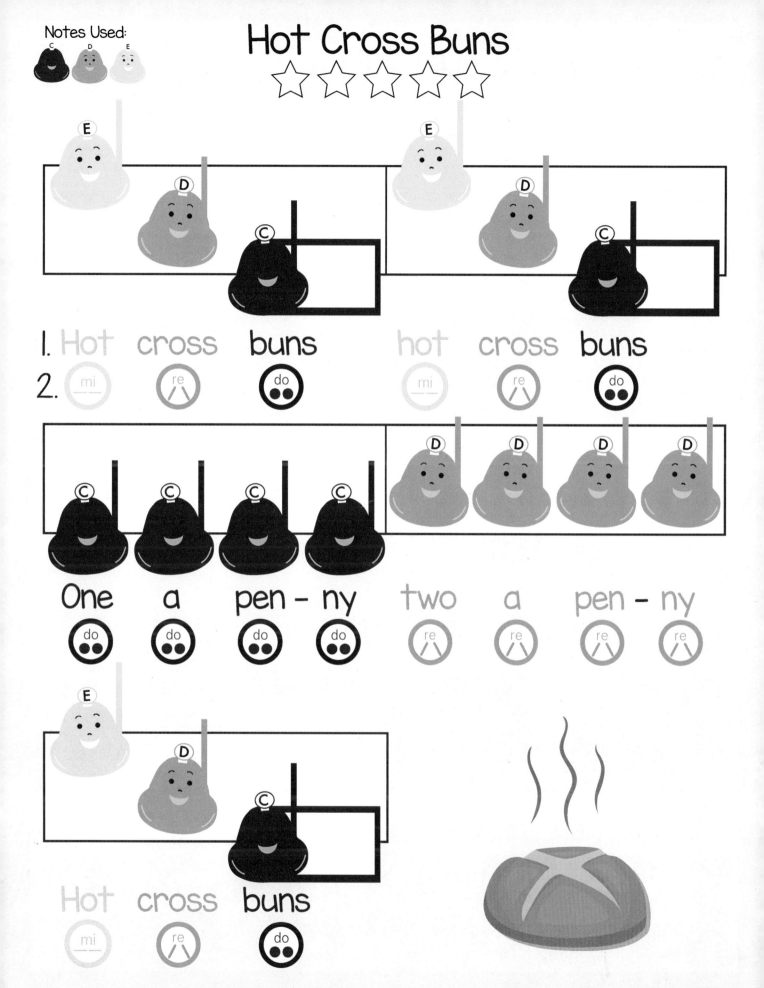

1. Hot   cross   buns   hot   cross   buns
2. mi   re   do   mi   re   do

One   a   pen - ny   two   a   pen - ny
do   do   do   do   re   re   re   re

Hot   cross   buns
mi   re   do

Mary Had a Little Lamb

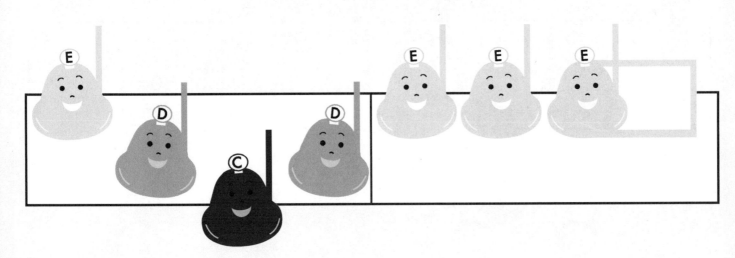

1. Ma – ry had a lit – tle lamb
2. Fol – lowed her to school one day
3.

(mi) (re) (do) (re) (mi) (mi) (mi)

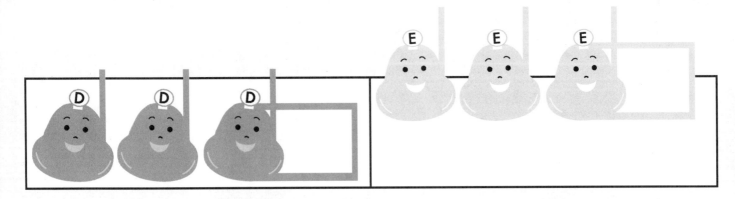

Lit – tle lamb   lit – tle lamb
school one day   school one day

(re) (re) (re)   (mi) (mi) (mi)

Ma - ry   **had**   a   lit - tle lamb whose
Fol - lowed **her**   to   school one day which

fleece was white as   **snow**
was   a - gainst the   **rules**

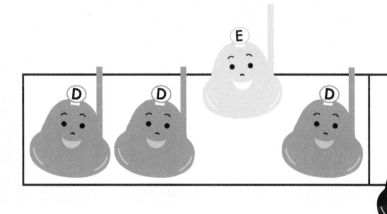

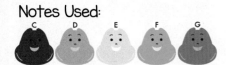
Notes Used:

Jingle Bells

☆ ☆ ☆ ☆ ☆

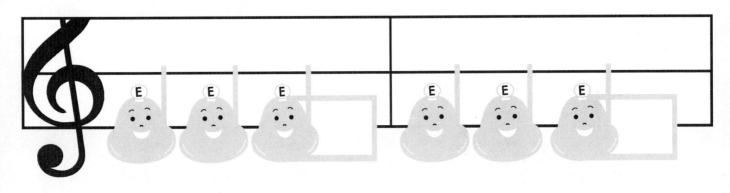

1. Jin - gle bells   jin - gle bells

2. mi mi mi   mi mi mi

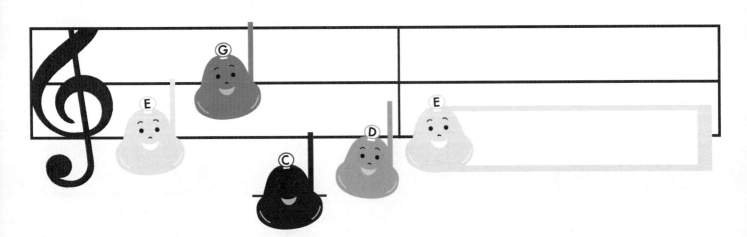

Jin - gle all the way

mi sol do re mi

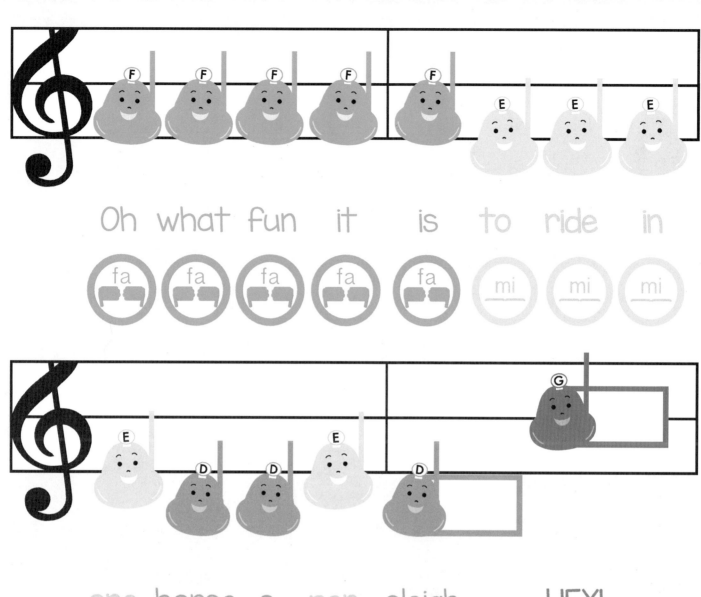

Oh what fun it is to ride in

one horse o - pen sleigh   HEY!

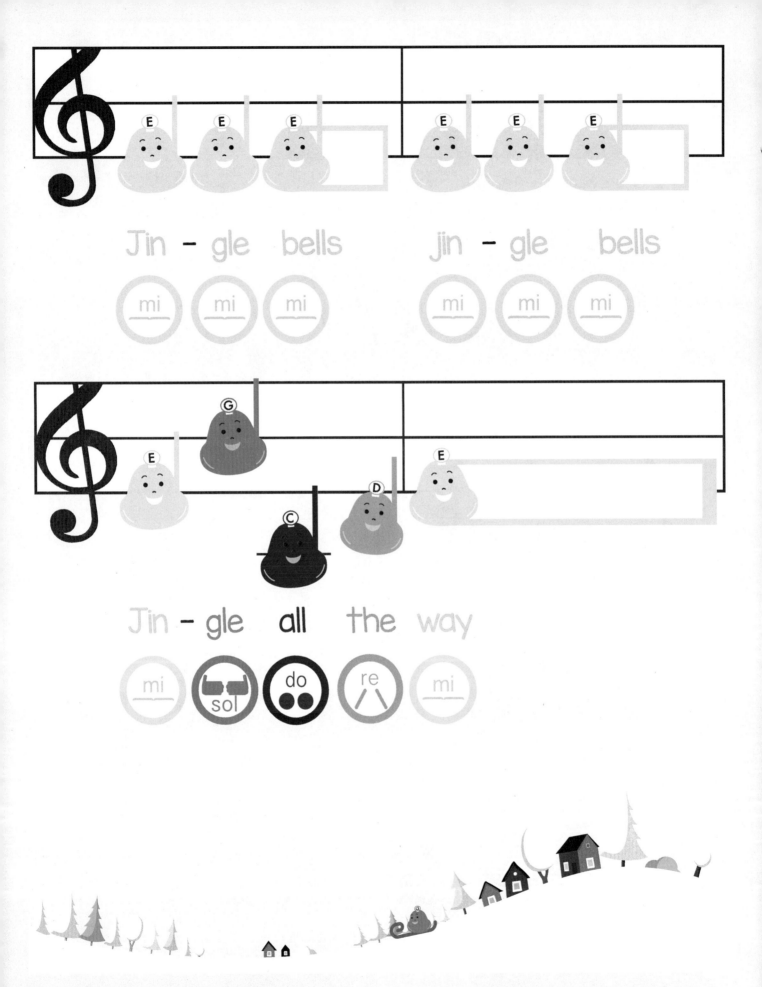

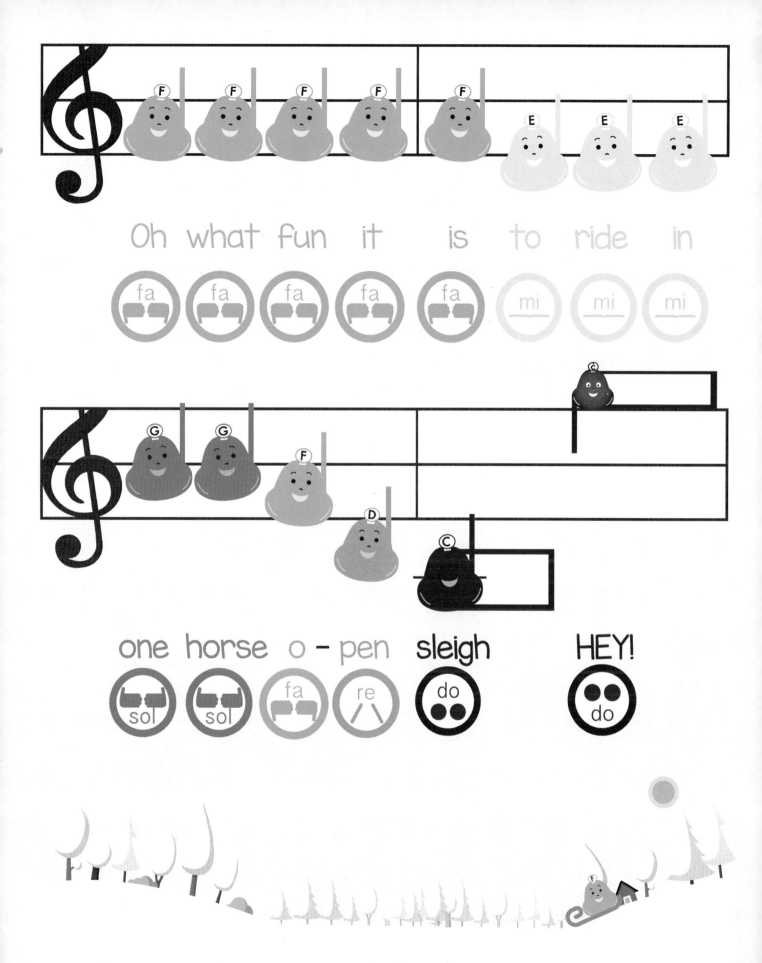

Twinkle Twinkle Little Star & The ABCs

☆☆☆☆☆

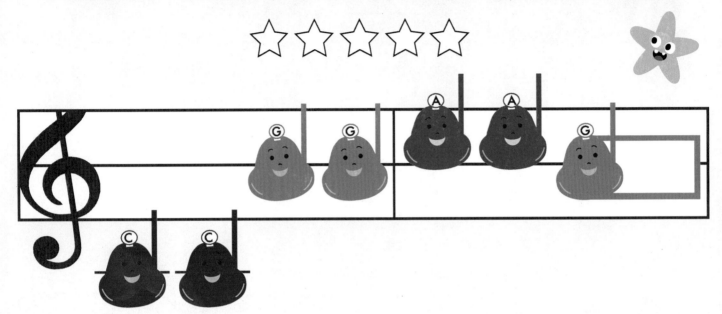

1. Twin - kle twin - kle   lit - tle   star
2. A   B   C   D   E   F   G
3. do   do   sol   sol   la   la   sol

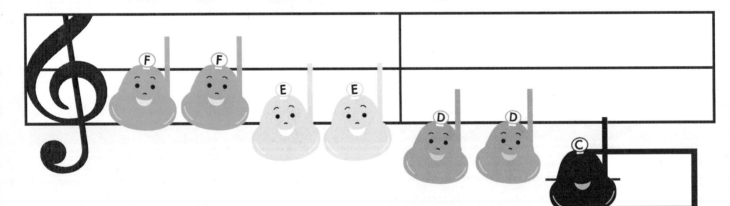

How I won-der what you **are**
H   I   J   K   L M N O **P**

fa   fa   mi   mi   re   re   **do**

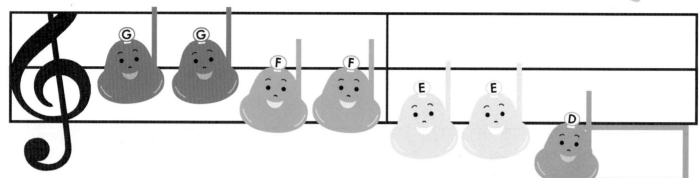

Up   a-bove the world so   high
Q   R   S   T   U   V

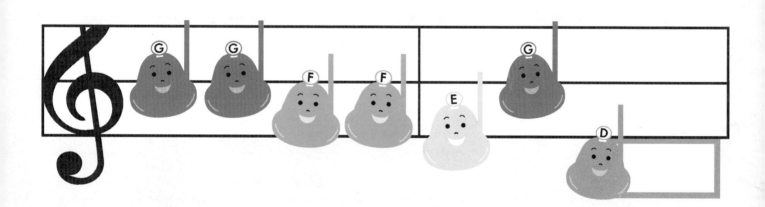

Like   a   dia-mond in   the   sky
W   X   Y   and   Z

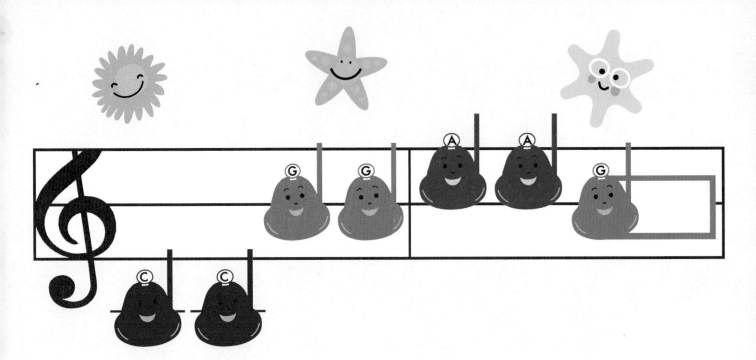

Twin - kle twin-kle lit - tle star
Now I know my A B Cs

do do sol sol la la sol

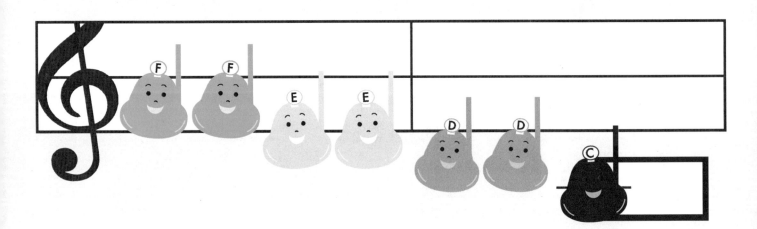

How I won - der what you are
Next time won't you sing with me

fa fa mi mi re re do

Ba Ba Black Sheep

☆☆☆☆☆

Ba ba black sheep, have you any wool?

Yes sir yes sir, three bags full.

One for my master, one for the dame.

One for the little boy that lives down the lane.

Ba ba black sheep, have you any wool?

Yes sir yes sir, three bags full.

The Farmer in the Dell

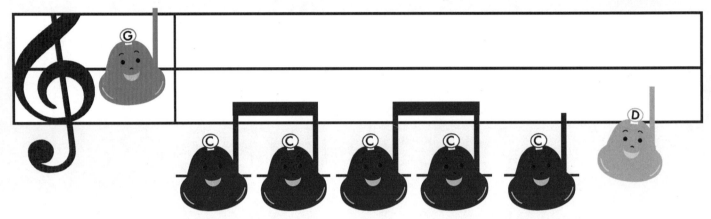

1. The farm-er in the dell the
2. The farm-er takes a wife the
3. sol do do do do do re

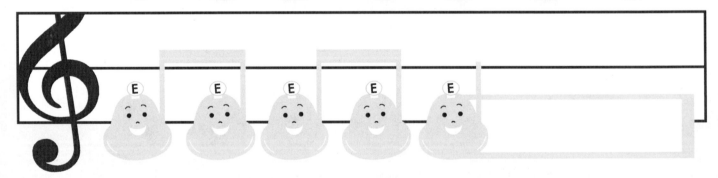

farm - er in the dell
farm - er takes a wife

mi mi mi mi mi

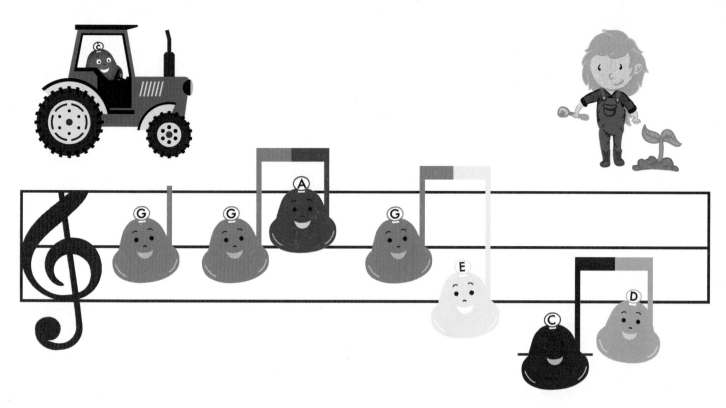

Heigh Ho the der - ry - o the
Heigh Ho the der - ry - o the

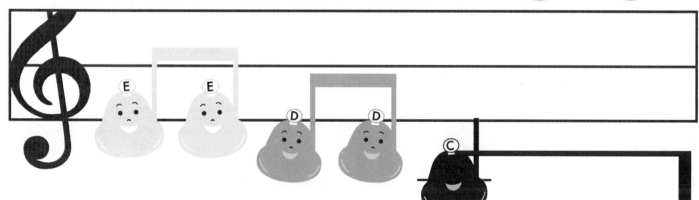

farm - er in the dell
farm - er takes a wife

Row Your Boat

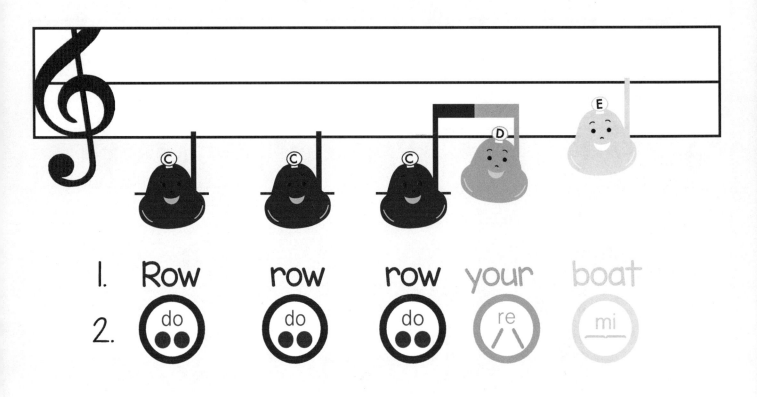

1. Row row row your boat
2. (do) (do) (do) (re) (mi)

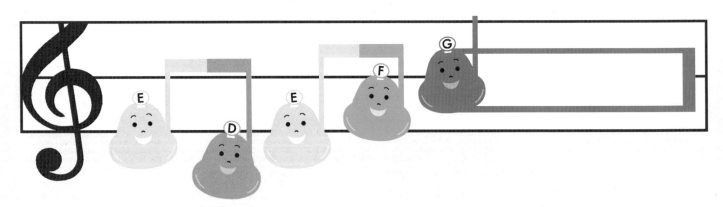

Gent - ly down the stream

mi   re   mi   fa   sol

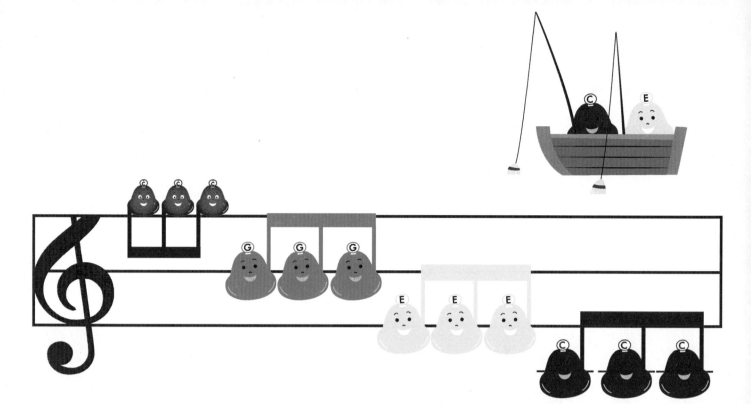

Mer-ri-ly mer-ri-ly mer-ri-ly mer-ri-ly

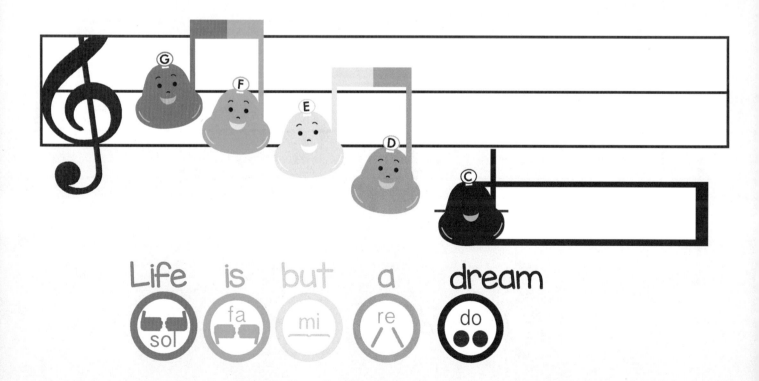

Life is but a dream

When The Saints Go Marching In
☆ ☆ ☆ ☆ ☆

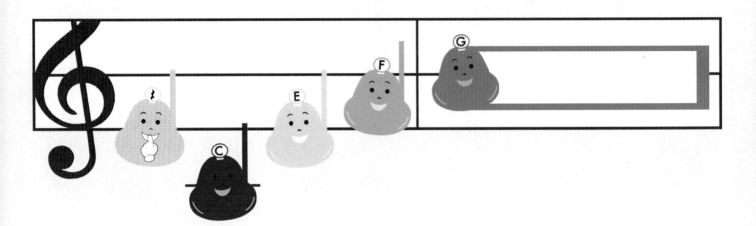

1. Rest   Oh   when   the   saints
2. Rest   do   mi   fa   sol

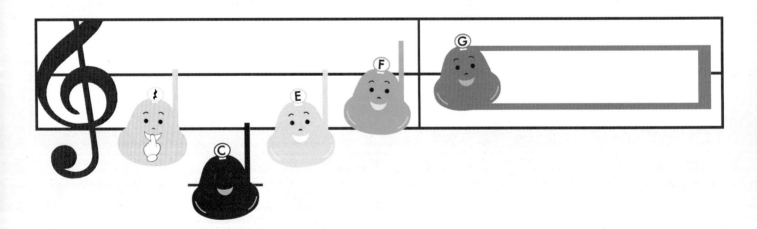

Rest   Oh   when   the   saints
Rest   do   mi   fa   sol

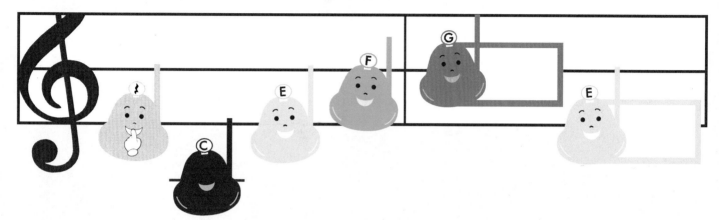

Rest   **Oh**   when   the   saints   go

Rest

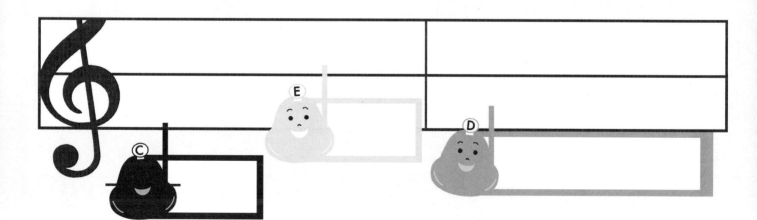

mar   -   ching   in

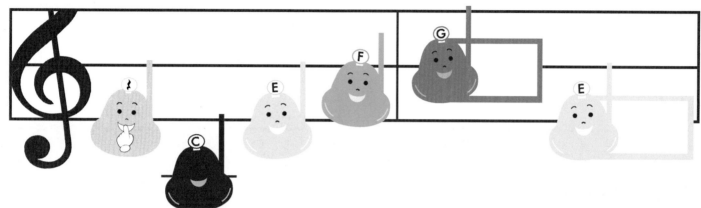

Rest **Oh** when the saints go

Rest do mi fa sol mi

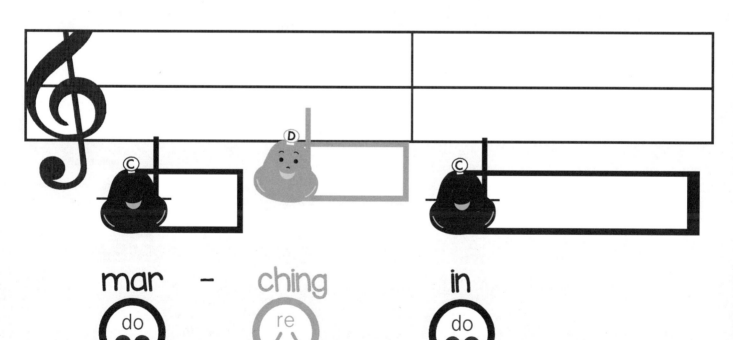

mar - ching in

do re do

On Top of Spaghetti

Note: This song only has
3 beats in each measure

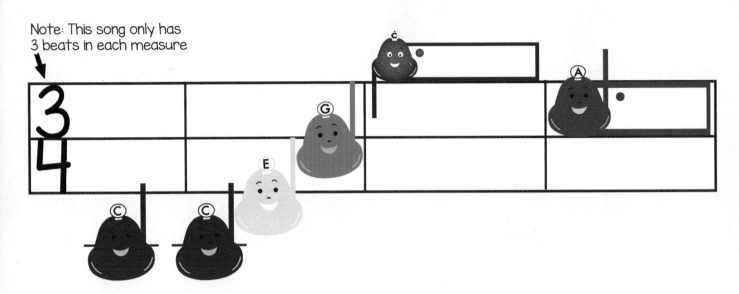

1. On   top   of   spa - ghet - ti
2. It   rolled off the   ta   - ble
3.

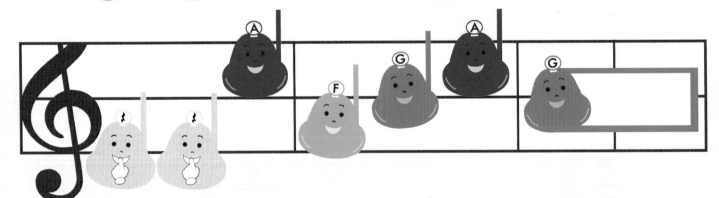

Rest Rest All co -vered in   cheese
Rest Rest And on   to   the floor

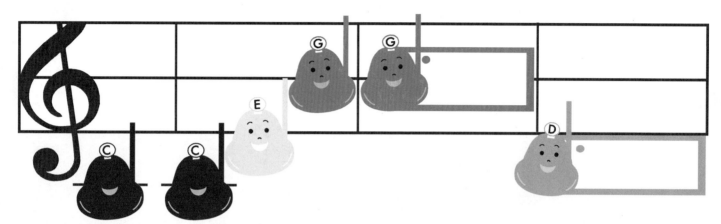

I lost my poor meat- ball
And then my poor meat- ball

do do mi sol sol re

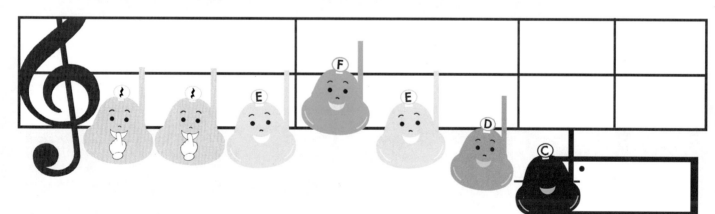

Rest Rest When some-bo - dy sneezed
Rest Rest It rolled out the door

mi fa mi re do

Are you Sleeping?

☆☆☆☆☆

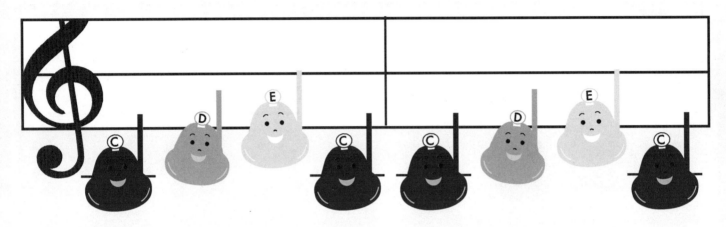

1. Are you sleep -ing are you sleep -ing
2. Fre - re Jac -ques fre - re Jac -ques
3.

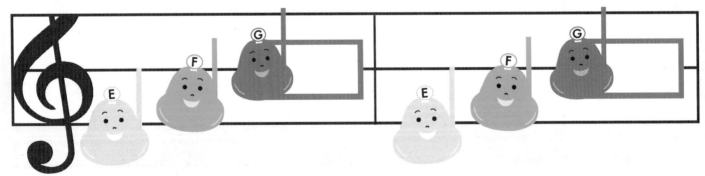

Bro -ther John   bro -ther John
Dor -mez-vous   dor -mez-vous

Morn-ing bells are ring-ing morn-ing bells are ring-ing
Son-nez les ma-ti-nes son-nez les ma-ti-nes

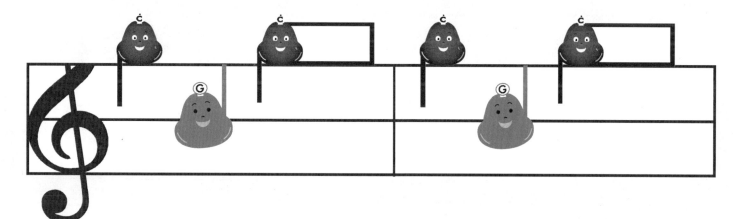

ding dang dong   ding dang dong!
ding dang dong   ding dang dong!

Sweet Beets

⭐☆☆☆☆

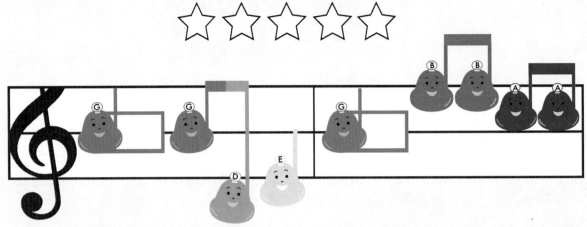

1. Sweet beets, we've got some. If you **want some**

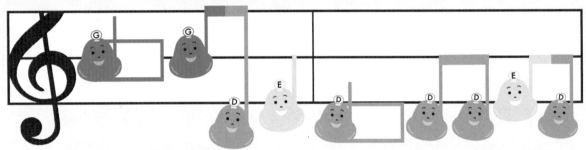

sweet beets, we got 'em. If you want some

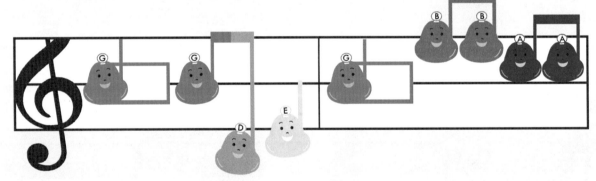

Sweet beets, we've got some. If you **want some**

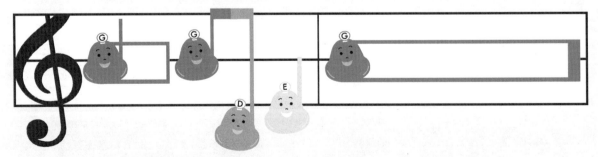

sweet beets, we got 'em.

Tap or clap the rhythms below

Note: the colors here mimic a popular rhythm manipulatve called Note Knacks. They do not indicate a specific note or pitch.

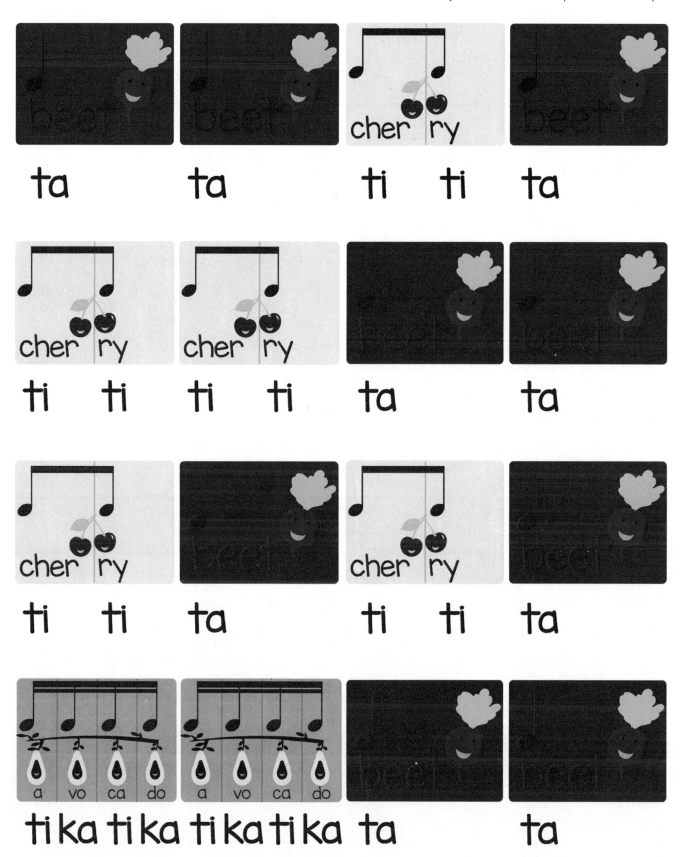

ta   ta   ti   ti   ta

ti   ti   ti   ti   ta   ta

ti   ti   ta   ti   ti   ta

ti ka ti ka ti ka ti ka   ta   ta

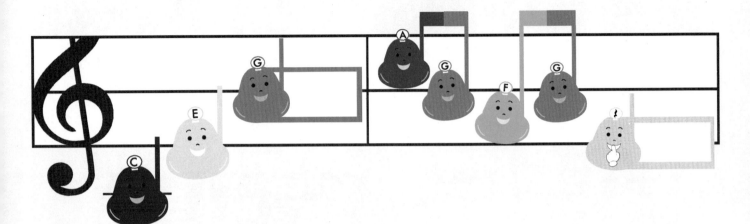

Avocado

Notes Used:

1. **Ah** Ah Aah a – vo – ca – do Rest
2. **Ah** Ah Aah a – gua – ca – te Rest
3.

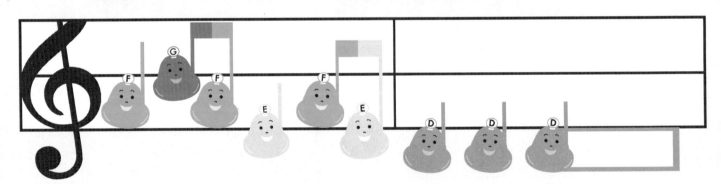

Woa **don't** you know that I love you so

me gus-**ta** mu-cho qui-eres comer?

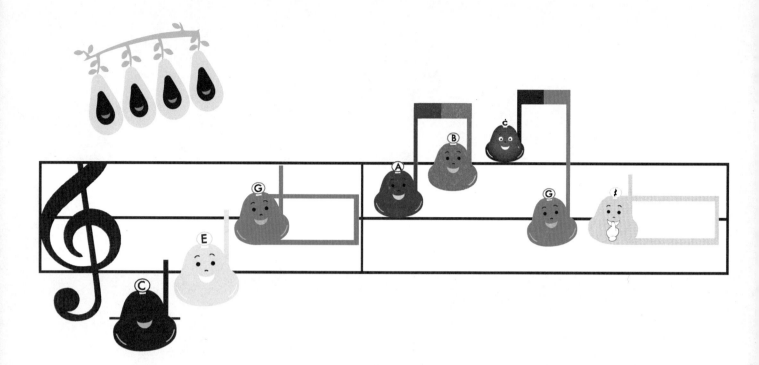

Ah   Ah   Aah   a‑vo‑ca‑do   Rest
Ah   Ah   Aah   a‑gua‑ca‑te   Rest

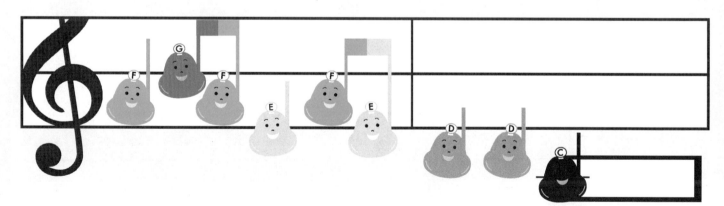

Woa **don't** you know that I   love you **so**
me gus‑**ta** mu‑cho I'd eat   it   all **day!**

Chapter 1

#1 Hello C

#2 Short and Long

#3 C and Shh

#4 Chord Watching

#5 Do-Mi-Sol Slide

#6 Solfege in C Major

CONGRATULATIONS

You completed My First Songbook Volume 1 and are now ready for Level 2.

Made in the USA
San Bernardino, CA
26 October 2016